WORLD SOCCER LEGENDS

THE WORLD'S GREATEST CLUBS

Abbeville Press Publishers

New York · London

Team rosters and statistics are current as of May 2019.

A portion of this book's proceeds are donated to the **Hugo Bustamante AYSO Playership Fund**, a national scholarship program to help ensure that no child misses the chance to play AYSO Soccer. Donations to the fund cover the cost of registration and a uniform for a child in need.

Text by Illugi Jökulsson
Design and layout: Árni Torfason

For the English-language edition
Editor: Matt Garczynski
Production manager: Louise Kurtz
Copy editor: Ashley Benning
Layout: Ada Rodriguez

PHOTOGRAPHY CREDITS

Shutterstock: pp. 6 (Fotografie K.J. Schraa), 7 (kivnl), 9 (Marco Canoniero), 10 (Alexandr Medvedkov), 11 (cristiano barni), 12 (Torres: kivnl), 12 (Godín: CosminIftode), 13 (Marco Canoniero), 14 (Iakov Filimonov), 15 (Jose Breton - Pics Action), 17 (Maxisport), 18 (Alexandr Medvedkov), 19 (Fingerhut), 20 (Lahm: CP DC PRESS), 20 (Müller: Mitch Gunn), 21 (daykung), 22 (Tupungato), 23 (CosminIftode), 24 (Reus: Jose Breton - Pics Action), 25 (Jose Breton - Pics Action), 26 (ARoxoPT), 27 (EFECREATA.COM), 28 (Deco: A.PAES), 26 (Hulk: CP DC Press), 29 (Bukharev Oleg), 30 (Sergio Monti Photography), 31 (Fabio Diena), 32 (Eto'o: Fabio Diena), 32 (Vieri: Paolo Bona), 32 (Cambiasso: Mitch Gunn), 33 (Marco Canoniero), 34 (MikeDotta), 35 (cristiano barni), 36 (Piero: Fabio Diena), 36 (Buffon: cristiano barni), 37 (cristiano barni), 39 (Oleksandr Osipov), 41 (Oleksandr Osipov), 42 (Alastair Wallace), 43 (Oleksandr Osipov), 44 (Silva: atatonia82), 45 (kivnl), 48 (Giggs: Fabio Diena), 49 (Jose Breton - Pics Action), 50 (PhotoLondonUK), 51 and back cover top (Mitch Gunn), 53 (Stefan Ugljevarevic), 54 (Alexandr Medvedkov), 55 (Oleksandr Osipov), 56 (Ronaldo: Maxisport), 56 (Zidane: Fabio Diena), 55 (Casillas: Marcos Mesa Sam Wordley), 57 (imagestockdesign), 58 (Silvi Photo), 59 (Ververidis Vasilis), 60 (Bale: Photo Works), 61 (MDI), 63 and back cover bottom (Jose Breton - Pics Action)

Getty Images: front cover (David S. Bustamante/Soccrates), pp. 8 (Basten: Bob Thomas), (Van Der Sar: Shaun Botterill), (Rijkaard: VI-Images), 16 (Ronaldinho: Ben Radford), 16 and back cover middle (Guardiola: Jasper Juinen), 16 (Cruyff: VI-Images), 20 (Beckenbauer: Hulton Archive), 36 (Platini: Getty Images / Staff), 40 (Suarez: Jamie McDonald), 40 (Gerrard: Laurence Griffiths), 44 (Touré: Alex Livesey), 47 (Bob Thomas), 48 (Charlton: Hulton Archive), 48 (Rooney: Shaun Botterill), 52 (Silva: Dean Mouhtaropoulos), 52 (Zlatan: Dean Mouhtaropoulos), 60 (Gascoigne: David Cannon), 60 (Lineker: Bob Thomas)

Wikimedia Commons: pp. 24 (Sammer: Bundesarchiv), 24 (Reuter: v mt7 - Eget arbete), 38 (By Ruaraidh Gillies - The revamped Main Stand Anfield, CC BY-SA 2.0), 40 (Clemence: By Marcel Antonisse / Anefo - Nationaal Archief), 46 (By Steve Collis from Melbourne, Australia)

Other: p. 44 (Bell: https://es.mancity.com)

First published in the United States of America in 2019 by Abbeville Press, 655 Third Avenue, New York, NY 10017

First Edition
10 9 8 7 6 5 4 3 2 1

ISBN 978-0-7892-1353-2

Library of Congress Cataloging-in-Publication Data available upon request

For bulk and premium sales and for text adoption procedures, write to Customer Service Manager, Abbeville Press, 655 Third Avenue, New York, NY 10017, or call 1-800-ARTBOOK.

Visit Abbeville Press online at www.abbeville.com.

CONTENTS

AFC AJAX

NETHERLANDS

FOUNDED: 1900

OFFICIAL NAME: AMSTERDAMSCHE FOOTBALL CLUB AJAX

NICKNAMES: DE GODENZONEN (SONS OF THE GODS)

HOME STADIUM: JOHAN CRUYFF ARENA

OPENED: 1996

CAPACITY: 54,990

RECORD ATTENDANCE: 54,874 (AGAINST REAL MADRID IN 2019)

Johan Cruyff Arena

HISTORY

Ajax was founded on March 18, 1900. The name was derived from a hero of Greek legend who fought in the Trojan War. The team debuted in the top league in 1911 and won its first KNVB Cup title in 1917. A year later, Ajax became league champion for the first time, defending the title in the following season. The team won the league five times in the 1930s, and from then on continued winning major titles here and there in the national league and cup tournaments.

However, the year 1965 would be a turning point for Ajax when Rinus Michels was hired as coach. Michels introduced a new system called Total Soccer and ushered in the longest victorious era in Ajax history with the help of players like Johan Cruyff. With Michels in command, the the team won four league titles, three cups, and in 1971, Ajax's first UEFA Champions League title (then known as the European Cup). Michels then moved on to coach Barcelona, though Ajax would remain European champions the next two years and maintain its winning streak at home as well.

Strong young players kept moving up from the team's youth academy, and the national titles kept piling up. In 1987, the team won the European Cup Winners' Cup and the UEFA Cup in 1992, led by Louis van Gaal. He was still at the helm in 1995 when the team conquered the top league, the Eredivisie, without losing a single game—a feat that remains unmatched by any other team. To crown the winning streak, Ajax won the UEFA Champions League in the same year, defeating AC Milan in the final. Ajax is the most successful team in Dutch history and also one of the world's most triumphant teams. According to the IFFHS, Ajax ranks seventh among the most successful teams of the 20th century.

Ajax player Frenkie de Jong during an Ajax—Feyenoord match.

FRENKIE DE JONG

Frenkie de Jong was only 18 when Ajax acquired him from the youth academy Willem II. Despite his age, he would soon become an integral player, usually as a defensive midfielder, with daring dribbling skills and remarkable game intelligence. In January 2019, the great powerhouse Barcelona announced that the team had acquired the young player, and he signed a contract calling for his transfer in July the same year. He is no doubt one of the world's most promising players.

TITLES

EREDIVISIE: 34
KVNB CUP: 19
JOHAN CRUYFF SHIELD: 8
UEFA CHAMPIONS LEAGUE: 4
UEFA CUP WINNERS' CUP: 1

UEFA EUROPA LEAGUE: 1
UEFA INTERTOTO CUP: 1
UEFA SUPER CUP: 2
INTERCONTINENTAL CUP: 2

MOST FAMOUS PLAYERS

MARCO VAN BASTEN

Though forced to retire at 28 due to injury, Marco van Basten scored a whopping 300 goals in his career. He is one of the greatest strikers of all time, having been awarded the sought-after Ballon d'Or three times. He was also named the best player of the 1988 UEFA Euro tournament, which he won with the Dutch national team. With Ajax, van Basten won the league three times and with AC Milan, he won the top Italian league another three.

EDWIN VAN DER SAR

It is safe to say goalkeeper Edwin van der Sar had a successful career, amassing a total of 27 titles, most with Ajax and Manchester United. He won the UEFA Champions League with both teams, first in 1995 and then 2008. Playing for Manchester United, van der Sar set a world record by not conceding a goal for 1,311 minutes. It is difficult to argue against the claim that Edwin van der Sar is one of the most talented goalkeepers of all time.

FRANK RIJKAARD

Considered by many to be the greatest defensive midfielders in history, Frank Rijkaard played an important part in Ajax's successes in the 1980s and '90s, helping the team win the 1995 Champions League tournament. Rijkaard also enjoyed a successful career with AC Milan. He won the European Championship with the Dutch national team in 1988. He later became coach of the national team and later Barcelona, steering the latter to victory in the 2006 Champions League final against Arsenal.

THE TEAM TODAY

Ajax has an ongoing rivalry with the Dutch teams PSV and Feyenoord. The team's latest Eredivisie victory came in 2019, after having landed in the league's top spots for nine consecutive seasons. Ajax also enjoyed its 19th cup victory, previously claimed by Ajax in 2010. Despite these achievements at home, the team's international performance has yet to reach its former glory, given that Dutch soccer has nowhere close to the same funds as the continent's top leagues.

Today, Ajax is viewed as one of the world's most exciting teams. The team made it to the semifinals of the 2019 Champions League, eliminating soccer giants Real Madrid and Juventus along the way. Ajax is populated by some of the most promising players of today, such as Matthijs de Ligt and Donny van de Beek. It will remain difficult for Ajax to keep these gifted players, but if the team manages to hold on to the core older players, and maintain its steady stream of strong prospects from the youth academy pouring into its ranks, it is certain that Ajax's future will remain a thrilling prospect.

Coach: Erik ten Hag

Erik ten Hag

GOALKEEPERS

24	Cameroon	André Onana
26	Greece	Kostas Lamprou
28	Portugal	Bruno Varela (on loan from Benfica)
33	Croatia	Dominik Kotarski

DEFENDERS

2	Denmark	Rasmus Nissen Kristensen
3	Netherlands	Joël Veltman
4	Netherlands	Matthijs de Ligt (captain)
8	Netherlands	Daley Sinkgraven
12	Morocco	Noussair Mazraoui
16	Argentina	Lisandro Magallán
17	Netherlands	Daley Blind
27	Netherlands	Perr Schuurs
31	Argentina	Nicolás Tagliafico

MIDFIELDERS

19	Morocco	Zakaria Labyad
20	Denmark	Lasse Schöne
—	Romania	Răzvan Marin
22	Morocco	Hakim Ziyech
6	Netherlands	Donny van de Beek
10	Serbia	Dušan Tadić
15	Netherlands	Carel Eiting
30	Netherlands	Dani de Wit

FORWARDS

7	Brazil	David Neres
9	Netherlands	Klaas-Jan Huntelaar
18	Burkina Faso	Hassane Bandé
25	Denmark	Kasper Dolberg
32	Czech Republic	Václav Černý

ATLÉTICO MADRID

SPAIN

FOUNDED: 1903

OFFICIAL NAME: CLUB ATLÉTICO DE MADRID

NICKNAMES: LOS COLCHONEROS (THE MATTRESS MAKERS), LOS ROJIBLANCOS (THE RED AND WHITES)

HOME STADIUM: WANDA METROPOLITANO

OPENED: 1994

CAPACITY: 67,829

RECORD ATTENDANCE: 67,804 (AGAINST REAL MADRID IN 2019)

Wanda Metropolitano

HISTORY

In 1903, the soccer club Athletic Club Sucursal de Madrid was established by Basque students as a youth division of their favorite team Athletic Bilbao. The teams wore similar uniforms, blue and white, but both had changed into striped white and red by 1911—colors that endure to this day. Legend has it that mattresses were produced in the white and red colors back then, so the unused leftover cloth could be turned into uniforms cheaply. In fact, Atlético Madrid is sometimes referred to as "the Mattress Makers."

The team grew apart from Bilbao in 1921 but it wasn't until 1947 that it became Club Atlético de Madrid. By then it had won the top league, La Liga, twice in 1940 and 1941.

The next two decades were kind to the team. In the years between 1950 and 1977, Atlético Madrid took an additional six La Liga titles, the Spanish Cup five times, the UEFA Cup Winners' Cup and then competed in the Champions League final (then known as the European Cup).

The controversial businessman and politician Jesús Gil took over as manager in 1987 and began injecting vast funds into the team. He also shut down the team's youth academy and made many other strange decisions. Performance was poor overall, and the team barely made it to La Liga in 1995, although they miraculously managed to claim the title a year later. At the end of 1999, the team's board was investigated on suspicion of fraud and Gil was fired. Atlético was relegated to the Segunda Division during the same season and spent the next two years there. After that the team moved on to greener pastures and finally won the league again in 2014. The team has now battled its way to the Champions League final twice in this decade.

Antoine Griezmann in Turin, Italy, on March 12, 2019 during the UEFA Champions League Round of 16 Second Leg match, Juventus vs. Atlético Madrid.

ANTOINE GRIEZMANN

All teams dream of having players such as Antoine Griezmann on board. This diligent and driven player can assume any forward position and manages to score a goal regardless of his location on the field. He was chosen as La Liga Best Player in 2016, Best FIFA Men's Player in the same year, and then 2018 Best FIFA Men's Player during the 2018 World Cup, won by France.

TITLES

LA LIGA: 10	UEFA EUROPA LEAGUE: 3
LA LIGA 2: 1	UEFA CUP WINNERS' CUP: 1
COPA DEL REY: 10	UEFA SUPER CUP: 3
SUPERCOPA DE ESPAÑA: 2	INTERCONTINENTAL CUP: 1

MOST FAMOUS PLAYERS

FERNANDO TORRES

Fernando Torres was just 17 years old when he played his first professional game for his youth club Atlético Madrid. And he scored his first goal only a week later. This great goal scorer continued racking them up, eventually being bought by Liverpool in 2007. Torres was a true fan favorite and broke a number of records: he is the fastest ever to score 50 goals for Liverpool. With Spain, he won two European Championship titles and the 2010 World Cup. Torres was awarded the Golden Boot in 2012.

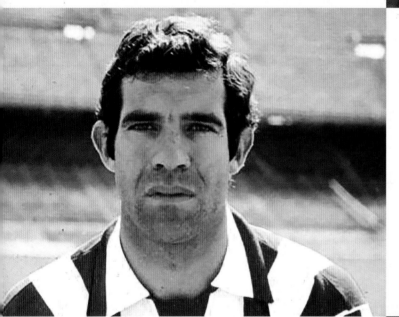

LUIS ARAGONÉS

Atlético can certainly boast of an abundance of talented forwards in its ranks over the years, but none has scored as many goals for the team as Luis Aragonés (with a total of 123 goals!). He was known for his free kick skills and, during the team's golden years, he won the top league three times as player and then again as coach in 1977. Aragonés led the Spanish national team to victory in the 2008 European Championship.

DIEGO GODÍN

They don't come any tougher than the Uruguayan player Diego Godín. The team captain has the most appearances by a foreigner in the team's history and has played a pivotal role in all of Atlético's titles over recent years. Despite his center back position, Godín regularly scores important goals, mostly as headers. Scoring aside, he is a true leader on the field and close to irreplaceable for the team as a whole.

THE TEAM TODAY

Atlético Madrid has long been considered Spain's third-best soccer club, following Barcelona and neighbors Real Madrid. At its best, Atlético Madrid can beat all the top teams and always puts up a good fight against Barcelona and Real in La Liga. Their 2014 and 2016 UEFA Champions League titles, as well as Europa League wins in 2010, 2012, and 2018, speak volumes regarding Atlético's European performance, proving that Atlético Madrid is among the world's best.

Coach Diego Simeone has led the team since 2011, and Atlético has blossomed under his guidance! The team plays dynamic and entertaining offensive soccer but also maintains a strong defensive bulwark for any attacking opponent wishing to break through to the goal. Many of the world's greatest forwards have played for the team in recent years, such as Fernando Torres, Sergio Agüero, Diego Costa and Radamel Falcao, to name a few.

Coach: Diego Simeone

Álvaro Morata

GOALKEEPERS

1	Spain	Antonio Adán
13	Slovenia	Jan Oblak

DEFENDERS

2	Uruguay	Diego Godín (captain)
3	Brazil	Filipe Luís
4	Colombia	Santiago Arias
15	Montenegro	Stefan Savić
18	Argentina	Nehuén Pérez
20	Spain	Juanfran
21	France	Lucas Hernandez
24	Uruguay	José Giménez

MIDFIELDERS

5	Ghana	Thomas Partey
6	Spain	Koke
8	Spain	Saúl
11	France	Thomas Lemar
14	Spain	Rodrigo
23	Spain	Vitolo

FORWARDS

7	France	Antoine Griezmann
9	Croatia	Nikola Kalinić
10	Argentina	Ángel Correa
19	Spain	Diego Costa
22	Spain	Álvaro Morata (on loan from Chelsea)

BARCELONA

SPAIN

FOUNDED: 1899

OFFICIAL NAME: FUTBOL CLUB BARCELONA

NICKNAMES: BARÇA AND BLAUGRANA

HOME STADIUM: CAMP NOU

OPENED: 1957

CAPACITY: 99,354

RECORD ATTENDANCE: 120,000 (AGAINST JUVENTUS IN 1986)

Camp Nou

HISTORY

In 1899, the Swiss soccer pioneer Hans Gamper advertised for players to join in founding a soccer club in Barcelona, which led to the establishment of Futbol Club Barcelona. The club viewed itself not only as a soccer team but a symbol for Catalonia, making Catalan the official language of the team early in the 20th century.

The team has been successful throughout most of its history, but it saw its biggest downturn in the late 1950s when construction of the team's new home stadium, the magnificent Camp Nou, left the team short of funds to purchase players. A pivotal year for the team came in 1979 when Barcelona acquired a farmhouse called La Masia for youth academy players. La Masia has since produced a number of the world's greatest soccer players, such as Pep Guardiola, Xavi, and of course legend Lionel Messi.

The investment paid off handsomely in the late 1980s and '90s when Johan Cruyff, a former member of the team, was hired as coach and the first generation of players graduated from La Masia. With these players, along with acquired international soccer stars and Cruyff at the helm, one of the greatest soccer teams of all time was created. Cruyff introduced the team to the Dutch Total Soccer system, characterized by dynamic passes and fluid play, where players have vast freedom in how they position themselves on the field. The system in fact still defines the team. While many other teams have attempted to copy it, no other has been able to match Barcelona's success.

LIONEL MESSI

Messi was born in Argentina but moved to Barcelona to train at the youth academy. At only 17, Messi played in his first game for the main team and has since become one of the world's greatest players, if not the very best. He has won the Ballon d'Or five times, is the top goal scorer in the history of the Spanish league, and he has beat countless records.

TITLES

LA LIGA: 25
COPA DEL REY: 30
SUPERCOPA DE ESPAÑA: 13
UEFA CHAMPIONS LEAGUE: 5
UEFA CUP WINNERS' CUP: 4
UEFA SUPER CUP: 5
FIFA CLUB WORLD CUP: 3

Lionel Messi of Barcelona with Arturo Vidal during the UEFA Champions League Round of 16 Second Leg match between FC Barcelona and Olympique Lyonnais at Camp Nou on March 13, 2019.

MOST FAMOUS PLAYERS

RONALDINHO

Many claim that the Brazilian legend Ronaldinho could have become the best player of all time, even better than his former teammate Lionel Messi. He won the Spanish league title twice with Barcelona and the UEFA Champions League once, as well as being elected the world's best player twice. Yet Ronaldinho's sometimes exuberant lifestyle prevented him from reaching the expected heights.

PEP GUARDIOLA

It was none other than Johan Cruyff who saw something special in Guardiola when he assigned him the role of midfielder and playmaker, the player who controls his team's offense, on the so-called "Dream Team." He was not the fastest or strongest player, but his technical gifts and cunning made him one of the world's greatest midfielders. Guardiola's deep understanding of the game has paid off in recent years, and he is considered one of the most successful coaches of all time.

JOHAN CRUYFF

Following eight titles in the Dutch league with Ajax, Johan Cruyff was acquired by Barcelona for a record sum. This tactical genius was the symbol for the Total Soccer system, which allowed Cruyff to maneuver into any position on the field. His technical skills and game intelligence blossomed with Barcelona, and it is no wonder that he was chosen the best European player of the century by the IFFHS.

THE TEAM TODAY

Despite losing some of the world's top players in recent years, Barcelona's triumphant streak is far from slowing down. The team has won the Spanish league two consecutive years as well as the Spanish Copa del Rey five years in a row! Barcelona's biggest supporters, Blaugranes, now eagerly await another Champions League title, especially given that the team's archenemy, Real Madrid, has won three times in the last four years, while Barcelona's last Champions League victory took place in 2015.

Barcelona continues to shape incredible young players in its academy, and as the fourth-richest soccer club in the world, the team can afford many talented international soccer stars. With top players in every position, one of the world's best soccer academies, and a massive fan base, it is safe to assume that Barcelona will remain in the upper echelons for years to come.

Coach: Ernesto Valverde

Luis Suárez

GOALKEEPERS

1	Germany	Marc-André ter Stegen
13	Netherlands	Jasper Cillessen

DEFENDERS

2	Portugal	Nélson Semedo
3	Spain	Gerard Piqué
6	France	Jean-Clair Todibo
15	France	Clément Lenglet
17	Colombia	Jeison Murillo
18	Spain	Jordi Alba
20	Spain	Sergi Roberto
23	France	Samuel Umtiti
24	Belgium	Thomas Vermaelen

MIDFIELDERS

4	Croatia	Ivan Rakitić
5	Spain	Sergio Busquets
7	Brazil	Philippe Coutinho
8	Brazil	Arthur
12	Brazil	Rafinha
14	Brazil	Malcom
16	Spain	Sergi Samper
19	Ghana	Kevin-Prince Boateng
21	Spain	Carles Aleñá
22	Chile	Arturo Vidal

FORWARDS

9	Uruguay	Luis Suárez
10	Argentina	Lionel Messi (captain)
11	France	Ousmane Dembélé

BAYERN MUNICH

GERMANY

FOUNDED: 1900

OFFICIAL NAME: FUSSBALL-CLUB BAYERN MÜNCHEN E. V.

NICKNAME: DER FCB (THE FCB)

HOME STADIUM: ALLIANZ ARENA

OPENED: 2005

CAPACITY: 75,000

RECORD ATTENDANCE: 75,000

Allianz Arena

HISTORY

At the end of the 19th century, a few members of the Munich gymnastics club began playing soccer, but when club administrators prohibited them from joining the official soccer association in Germany, the players founded a new team, FC Bayern München. The team became successful almost immediately in southern Germany, taking home the first national championship title in 1932.

When the Nazis rose to power in Germany, both the president of the team and the coach were forced to flee due to their Jewish ancestry. Bayern Munich continued to struggle during the Nazi regime, and it took a long while for the team to recuperate following the end of WWII. Thirteen coaches were hired and fired in the years between 1945 and 1963! However, the team managed to win the DFB Cup for the first time in 1955. When the national soccer league was established in 1963, combining Germany's top five leagues, Bayern Munich didn't make the cut because 1860 München was considered a superior team and the Bundesliga only accepted one team from each city.

Two years later, Bayern Munich won the right to participate in the Bundesliga, sporting a team full of tremendous players such as Franz Beckenbauer, Gerd Müller, and Sepp Maier. The trio would later play a vital role in the "golden years" team, which went on to triumph both at home and across Europe over the next 15 years. The team fell into a minor slump in the 1980s and '90s but since then Bayern Munich has risen to become Germany's most successful soccer club.

MANUEL NEUER

Bayern Munich has had several of the world's best goalkeepers in its ranks, and that Manuel Neuer is often considered the best of bunch (even better than Sepp Maier and Oliver Kahn) says much about his level of skill. Neuer is known for moving out of the penalty area to clear away long passes from the defensive line, but he also excels inside the box and his ability to stop close-range shots is impeccable. He was chosen the best goalkeeper in the world four consecutive years, and some say that he deserved even more.

Manuel Neuer during a Bundesliga match between FC Schalke 04 & FC Bayern Munich, final score 0—4, on September 21, 2013, in Schalke, Germany.

TITLES

BUNDESLIGA: 28	UEFA CUP: 1
DFB-POKAL: 18	UEFA CUP WINNERS' CUP: 1
DFL-SUPERCUP: 7	UEFA SUPER CUP: 1
DFL-LIGAPOKAL: 6	INTERCONTINENTAL CUP: 2
UEFA CHAMPIONS LEAGUE: 5	FIFA CLUB WORLD CUP: 1

MOST FAMOUS PLAYERS

FRANZ BECKENBAUER

The Emperor, as Franz Beckenbauer was often dubbed, was one of the most powerful leaders to have ever graced the soccer field. Beckenbauer is one of the greatest midfielders in history, and his numerous titles and honors speak volumes to that effect. He is one of three players to have won the FIFA World Cup as both player and coach, and as member of Bayern Munich, Beckenbauer clinched the league title five times and won the Champions League three times, to list but a few accolades.

PHILIPP LAHM

Philipp Lahm is so talented that he can play at left back midfield just as easily as at right, and sometimes in the position of defensive midfielder. His leadership skills, however, were properly allowed to shine in 2013 when as team captain he led Bayern Munich to victory in the Champions League, DFB Cup, and the Bundesliga. Speed, stamina, and passing skills are only a few of the abilities that have made him into one of the world's top midfielders.

THOMAS MÜLLER

At only 20, Thomas Müller won the Ballon d'Or during the 2010 World Cup, where he was also chosen the Best Young Player. Germany came in third place in the tournament that year, but Müller helped the national team win the World Cup four years later. He was named the second-best player and received the Silver Boot. Meanwhile, Müller won the Championship League with Bayern, with seven league titles under his belt. He is generally positioned close to the opponent's goal, but he can also assume diverse forward positions, with one thing always certain: Müller always gives 100% for his team.

THE TEAM TODAY

Bayern Munich holds somewhat of a monopoly in the German league nowadays. Since 2013, the team has come out on top of the Bundesliga each year and won the DFB Cup three times. Bayern Munich is also well-off financially, allowing it to acquire the best players from its main opponents. For example, the team managed to snatch Mario Götze and Robert Lewandowski from the clutches of their great rivals in Dortmund.

Bayern Munich has also been successful in the UEFA Champions League, winning in 2013 and since then always managing to get to the playoff round, until 2018, when the team lost to Liverpool during the Round of 16. Bayern Munich will most likely continue to amass trophies in Germany while the team's supporters cross their fingers for the seventh Championship League trophy.

James Rodríguez

Coach: Niko Kovač

GOALKEEPERS

1	Germany	Manuel Neuer (captain)
26	Germany	Sven Ulreich
36	Germany	Christian Früchtl
39	Germany	Ron-Thorben Hoffmann

DEFENDERS

4	Germany	Niklas Süle
5	Germany	Mats Hummels
8	Spain	Javi Martínez
13	Brazil	Rafinha
17	Germany	Jérôme Boateng
27	Austria	David Alaba
32	Germany	Joshua Kimmich

MIDFIELDERS

6	Spain	Thiago
7	France	Franck Ribéry
10	Netherlands	Arjen Robben
11	Colombia	James Rodríguez (on loan from Real Madrid)
18	Germany	Leon Goretzka
19	Canada	Alphonso Davies
22	Germany	Serge Gnabry
24	France	Corentin Tolisso
29	France	Kingsley Coman
35	Portugal	Renato Sanches

FORWARDS

9	Poland	Robert Lewandowski
20	South Korea	Jeong Woo-yeong
25	Germany	Thomas Müller

BORUSSIA DORTMUND

GERMANY

FOUNDED: 1909

OFFICIAL NAME: BALLSPIELVEREIN BORUSSIA 09 E.V. DORTMUND

NICKNAMES: DIE BORUSSEN, DIE SCHWARZGELBEN (THE BLACK AND YELLOWS)

HOME STADIUM: SIGNAL IDUNA PARK

OPENED: 1974

CAPACITY: 81,365

RECORD ATTENDANCE: 83,000 (VARIOUS GAMES IN 2004)

Signal Iduna Park

HISTORY

In December 1909, a group of 18 young men assembled in a Dortmund bar to found a new soccer team. They borrowed the name from a local beer brand, and so Borussia Dortmund came into being. The term Borussia is Latin for Prussia, which Dortmund belonged to during that time. The team performed rather poorly to begin with and was eventually dissolved by the Allies after WWII like many other German organizations. A new team emerged as a result, Ballspielverein Borussia.

The team's performance improved, and Dortmund landed its first national title in 1956. The team won again the following year and then again in 1963, in the same year that the Bundesliga was established. Dortmund naturally won its place in the league, but the team was forced to wait until 1995 for a championship despite coming close several times. Dortmund was however the first German team to win a major European tournament, with the European Cup Winners' Cup in 1966.

The 1990s saw what is often considered the golden age of Dortmund where the team won the Bundesliga twice and then defeated Juventus in the 1997 Champions League final. Since then, the team has acquired another three German championship trophies, won the DFB Cup three times, and made it once to the Champions League final, where it lost 1–2 against another German team, Bayern Munich.

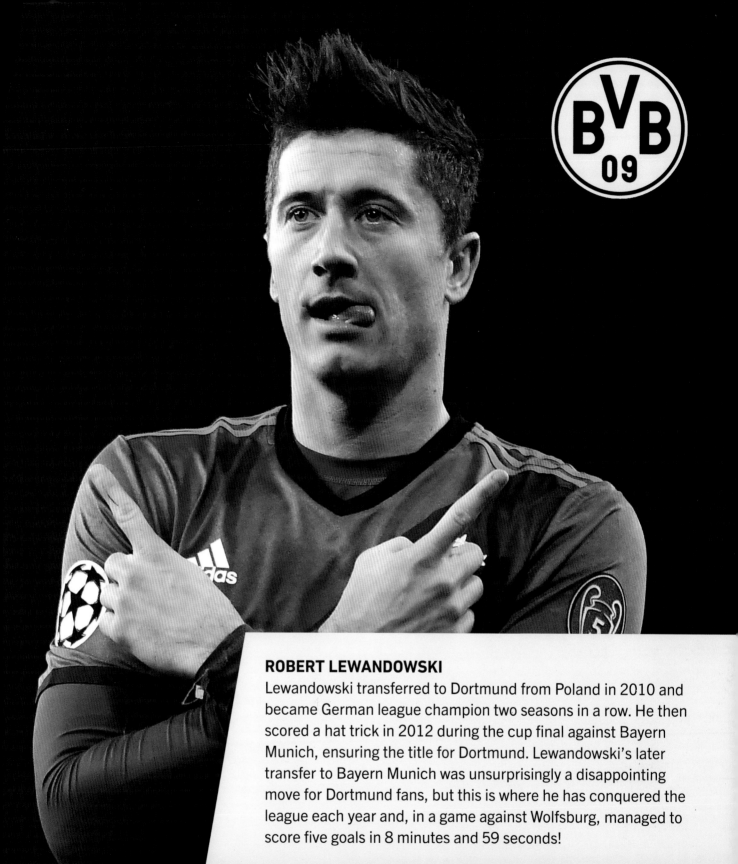

ROBERT LEWANDOWSKI

Lewandowski transferred to Dortmund from Poland in 2010 and became German league champion two seasons in a row. He then scored a hat trick in 2012 during the cup final against Bayern Munich, ensuring the title for Dortmund. Lewandowski's later transfer to Bayern Munich was unsurprisingly a disappointing move for Dortmund fans, but this is where he has conquered the league each year and, in a game against Wolfsburg, managed to score five goals in 8 minutes and 59 seconds!

Robert Lewandowski celebrates after a goal scored during the UEFA Champions League Round of 16 game between Arsenal FC and Bayern Munich at Emirates Stadium.

TITLES
BUNDESLIGA: 8
DFB-POKAL: 4
DFL-SUPERCUP: 5

UEFA CHAMPIONS LEAGUE: 1
UEFA CUP WINNERS' CUP: 1
INTERCONTINENTAL CUP: 1

MOST FAMOUS PLAYERS

MATTHIAS SAMMER

Sammer was chosen the world's best player in 1996. As captain of the Dortmund team, he had won the Bundesliga two consecutive years as well as winning the Euro 96 with the German national team. The following year, Sammer took home the UEFA Champions League title, and in 2002 he was the first ever Dortmund player to accomplish this feat as both player and coach. Sammer played first as defensive midfielder and then as sweeper, but he was always an accomplished goal scorer as well.

MARCO REUS

Dortmund's current captain was part of the team's youth training system, but began his Bundesliga career with Rot Weiss Ahlen. From there Reus transferred to Borussia Mönchengladbach and went on to ensure a place for the team in the 2012 UEFA Champions League, but Reus ended up not playing for Mönchengladbach that season because he had already returned to his original home in Dortmund. Reus's career has been plagued by frequent injuries but on a good day, Reus, and forward Mario Götze make up one of the fiercest attacking duos in Germany.

STEFAN REUTER

Reuter began his career with FC Nürnberg but transferred to Bayern Munich where he became a German champion twice. After a brief stint with Juventus in Italy, Reuter joined Dortmund and won the Bundesliga three times and then the UEFA Champions League, the first time in the team's history. This energetic winger, who played as a defender and midfielder with equal grace, was also part of the national team when Germany was crowned world champions in 1990 and European champions in 1996.

THE TEAM TODAY

Borussia Dortmund has been Bayern Munich's main competitor for the German championship title, which the latter has monopolized in recent years. Dortmund won the Bundesliga in 2012 and since then the team has landed in second place three times. Dortmund won the DFB Cup in 2012 and 2017, but many supporters hope that the team, or at the very least anyone aside from Bayern Munich, will win the Bundesliga title just to inject some life back into German soccer.

Borussia Dortmund can, however, boast that its games have the biggest attendance in the world. Its stadium of Signal Iduna Park has a capacity of almost 82,000, with every seat taken during home games. And the atmosphere during games is legendary, where the Die Gelbe Wand (The Yellow Wall), as the supporters are called, flank the south terrace and put fear into every Dortmund opponent.

Coach: Lucien Favre

Lucien Favre

GOALKEEPERS		
1	Switzerland	Roman Bürki
35	Switzerland	Marwin Hitz
40	Germany	Eric Oelschlägel

DEFENDERS		
2	France	Dan-Axel Zagadou
4	France	Abdou Diallo
5	Morocco	Achraf Hakimi (on loan from Real Madrid)
13	Portugal	Raphaël Guerreiro
16	Switzerland	Manuel Akanji
18	Argentina	Leonardo Balerdi
26	Poland	Łukasz Piszczek
29	Germany	Marcel Schmelzer
36	Turkey	Ömer Toprak

MIDFIELDERS		
6	Denmark	Thomas Delaney
7	England	Jadon Sancho
10	Germany	Mario Götze
17	Spain	Sergio Góme
19	Germany	Mahmoud Dahoud
22	United States	Christian Pulisic (on loan from Chelsea)
28	Belgium	Axel Witsel
33	Germany	Julian Weigl

FORWARDS		
9	Spain	Paco Alcácer
11	Germany	Marco Reus (captain)
20	Germany	Maximilian Philipp
27	Germany	Marius Wolf
34	Denmark	Jacob Bruun Larsen

FC PORTO

PORTUGAL

FOUNDED: 1893

OFFICIAL NAME: FUTEBOL CLUBE DO PORTO

NICKNAMES: AZUIS E BRANCOS (BLUE AND WHITES), DRAGÕES (DRAGONS)

HOME STADIUM: ESTÁDIO DO DRAGÃO

OPENED: 2003

CAPACITY: 50,083

RECORD ATTENDANCE: 52,000 (AGAINST BARCELONA 2003)

Estádio do Dragão

HISTORY

António Nicolau de Almeida, a Portuguese port wine merchant, fell in love with soccer on his travels around England and decided to found a soccer club in 1893 when he returned to his home city of Porto, naming it Futebol Clube do Porto. The team won numerous titles in the Porto district during its first years, and then joined a new nationwide soccer league when it was established in 1921. Porto won the first major title of the inaugural tournament, but only managed three more titles. The last one arrived in 1937, before a new national soccer tournament was founded in 1938. Once again, Porto won the first title of the tournament's inaugural season, and defended the title the following year.

A long drought began after that, and Porto wouldn't see another title for 16 years, when it won both the top league and cup titles. The newfound winning streak would be cut short,

and the team's performance once again plummeted. Aside from one cup title, Porto advanced little until 1977. That year brought another cup title, and a league trophy followed in 1978. Porto grew stronger in Europe and performed well in the Europe Cup Winners' Cup. The team made the finals of the same tournament in 1984, where it lost to Juventus. In 1987, Porto won its first major European title by defeating Bayern Munich 2–1 in the European Cup final (later becoming the UEFA Champions League). Porto didn't lose a single league game during the 2010–2011 and 2012–2013 seasons, making the team the second best in Portugal's history and the most successful Portuguese team in Europe.

Falcao during a Spanish Cup match between Valencia CF and AT Madrid, on November 3, 2012, in Mestalla Stadium, Valencia, Spain.

RADAMEL FALCAO

The Colombian Radamel Falcao is not only Porto's all-time top goal scorer in European tournaments, but also holds the record for most goals in international competitions in one season, scoring 17 goals in Porto's victory in the 2011 Europa League. Falcao won the Europa League again in 2012, then with Atlético Madrid. Today he captains Monaco, which won the French league in 2017.

TITLES

PRIMEIRA LIGA: 28

TAÇA DE PORTUGAL: 16

SUPERTAÇA CÂNDIDO DE OLIVEIRA: 21

UEFA CHAMPIONS LEAGUE: 2

UEFA EUROPA LEAGUE: 2

UEFA SUPER CUP: 1

INTERCONTINENTAL CUP: 2

MOST FAMOUS PLAYERS

DECO

There are not many players who have won the Champions League with two different teams, but Deco did, with Porto in 2004, when he was named the Man of the Match, and again in 2006 with Barcelona. Deco was born and raised in Brazil, but he received Portuguese citizenship in 2002 and chose to play for the Portuguese national team. This cunning midfielder has won 20 titles, 10 of these with Porto.

HULK

His full name is Givanildo Vieira de Sousa but it's the nickname "Hulk" that appears on the back of his jersey. People started calling him Hulk due to his resemblance to the actor Lou Ferrigno, who played the superhero in the TV series. The Hulk began his career at home in Brazil before traveling to Japan. He then joined Porto, where he went on to win a total of 10 titles, among them the Europa League in 2011. He was acquired by Zenit in Russia, won both the league and cup with the team, and now plays in China.

FERNANDO GOMES

Fernando Gomes was considered a technically skilled player at best, but when it came to positioning himself in the opponent's penalty box, he excelled. It was precisely this talent that made him Porto's top goal-scorer of all time, with 347 goals in 455 games! Nuno Gomes, another magnificent Portuguese forward, chose the last name as his nickname because of his admiration for Fernando.

THE TEAM TODAY

At home, Porto continues to collect trophies while facing tough competition from Benfica and Sporting CP. Porto won the league in 2018 and has not fallen below third place since 1976! However, the team has failed to claim the Portuguese Cup since 2011 and has yet to repeat its European victories, but should be happy with placing in the quarterfinals of the Champions League, as was the case in 2015 and 2019. Porto doesn't have the same funds as other big European teams, yet the team was named the 11th best soccer team in Europe for 2017—2018.

Coach: Sérgio Conceição

GOALKEEPERS

1	Spain	Iker Casillas
26	Brazil	Vaná
31	Portugal	Diogo Costa
40	Brazil	Fabiano

DEFENDERS

2	Uruguay	Maxi Pereira
3	Brazil	Éder Militão
4	Portugal	Diogo Leite
12	Portugal	Wilson Manafá
13	Brazil	Alex Telles
19	DR Congo	Chancel Mbemba
23	Brazil	João Pedro
28	Brazil	Felipe
33	Portugal	Pepe

MIDFIELDERS

6	Portugal	Bruno Costa
10	Spain	Óliver Torres
15	Senegal	Mamadou Loum (on loan from Braga)
16	Mexico	Héctor Herrera (captain)
22	Portugal	Danilo Pereira
25	Brazil	Otávio

FORWARDS

7	Portugal	Hernâni
8	Algeria	Yacine Brahimi
9	Cameroon	Vincent Aboubakar
11	Mali	Moussa Marega
14	Chad	Marius Mouandilmadji
17	Mexico	Jesús Corona
20	Spain	Adrián López
21	Portugal	André Pereira
29	Brazil	Francisco Soares
37	Brazil	Fernando Andrade

Iker Casillas

INTER MILAN

ITALY

FOUNDED: 1908

OFFICIAL NAME: FOOTBALL CLUB INTERNAZIONALE MILANO S.P.A.

NICKNAMES: I NERAZZURRI (THE BLACK AND BLUES), LA BENEAMATA (THE CHERISHED ONE)

HOME STADIUM: SAN SIRO

OPENED: 1926

CAPACITY: 80,018

RECORD ATTENDANCE: 83,381 (AGAINST SCHALKE IN 1997)

San Siro

HISTORY

The founders of the soccer team chose the name Football Club Internazionale because they wanted both native Italians as well as foreign players to feel welcome. It was always intended to be an international club. This was in the year 1908, and two years later the team won the first national league title. Inter, as supporters like to call the team, then won another championship title 10 years later. However, during the fascist regime, the team was merged with Unione Sportiva Milanese, and a few name changes would follow over the years. The team won the cup in 1939 and the league a year later. Its original name was then restored after WWII ended.

Inter Milan forged ahead and gathered further championship titles, the 1960s being particularly successful. Led by the tactical genius Helenio Herrera, it played a highly structured defensive game with bursting counterattacks. Using this system, the team won the league twice, the Italian Cup twice, and the European Cup twice. Inter has since maintained its winning streak with a minor slump in the '90s, the only decade in the team's history when it never won the league. However, the team certainly made up for this and went on to take the league five years in a row in the years between 2006 and 2010. In 2010, Inter also claimed both the cup and league titles, the team's only treble.

JAVIER ZANETTI

It is telling that the player with most game appearances for the international team Inter Milan is not an Italian, but in fact a South American player: the Argentine Javier Zanetti. Between 1995 and 2014, this versatile player appeared in 858 games for Inter and won a total of 16 major titles! When Zanetti retired, the team decided that his number 4 jersey should also be retired, and no player has used the number since.

Javier Zanetti celebrates after a goal against AC Milan in 2013.

TITLES

SERIE A: 18
COPPA ITALIA: 7
SUPERCOPPA ITALIANA: 5
UEFA CHAMPIONS LEAGUE: 3

UEFA EUROPA LEAGUE: 3
INTERCONTINENTAL CUP: 2
FIFA CLUB WORLD CUP: 1

MOST FAMOUS PLAYERS

SAMUEL ETO'O

Cameroonian Samuel Eto'o became the second player in history to score a goal in two Champions League finals. He won the tournament in 2006 and 2009 with Barcelona, managing the amazing treble (league, cup, and European competition) in 2009. He also became the first player to win all three two years in a row, after joining Inter Milan in 2010. Eto'o was named African Player of the Year four times, in 2003, 2004, 2005, and 2010. He also won Olympic Gold in 2000 with the Cameroon national team.

CHRISTIAN VIERI

The Italian forward Christian Vieri was the world's most expensive player when Inter acquired him from Lazio for almost 36 million dollars. Vieri would never stay with teams for long, but he played 143 games with Inter and scored 103 goals. He could score goals of every possible type, being both quick and strong, and was particularly fierce with headers, holding the record for most headed goals in the top Italian league.

ESTEBAN CAMBIASSO

Esteban Cambiasso began his career with Argentinos Juniors in Argentina but joined Real Madrid at a young age. However, it was with Inter Milan that his career really took off, and he amassed a total of 21 titles. Considered by many to be the world's most underappreciated player in the top league, Serie A, Cambiasso was a diligent and powerful player, creative on offense, and though he was most fruitful as a box-to-box midfielder, he could also assume a diversity of positions on the field with equal grace.

THE TEAM TODAY

Since winning the cup in 2011, Inter Milan has performed rather poorly. The team has made it no further than fourth place in the league and has often been eliminated before even reaching quarter- or semifinals in the Italian Cup. The same applies to the team's performance in Europe. The furthest Inter reached was the Round of 16 of the Champions League. The decline can be explained partially by changes in ownership over recent years, with several investors buying major shares and then selling them, while the team itself has hired and fired numerous coaches.

Inter Milan is nevertheless a legendary team with a vast fan base and can always boast that it is the only Italian team that has always played in the top league. No doubt, the seas will calm in the coming years. The dynamic Luciano Spalletti has led the team since 2017, and it seems like he is already steering toward brighter horizons. Internazionale supporters cross their fingers and hope that Inter can perhaps stop the victorious march of Juventus, which according to fans, has been dominant for way too long.

Coach: Luciano Spalletti

GOALKEEPERS

1	Slovenia	Samir Handanović (captain)
27	Italy	Daniele Padelli
46	Italy	Tommaso Berni
93	Italy	Raffaele Di Gennaro

DEFENDERS

2	Croatia	Šime Vrsaljko (on loan from Atlético Madrid)
6	Netherlands	Stefan de Vrij
13	Italy	Andrea Ranocchia
18	Ghana	Kwadwo Asamoah
21	Portugal	Cédric (on loan from Southampton)
23	Brazil	Miranda
29	Brazil	Dalbert
33	Italy	Danilo D'Ambrosio
37	Slovakia	Milan Škriniar

MIDFIELDERS

5	Italy	Roberto Gagliardini
8	Uruguay	Matías Vecino
14	Belgium	Radja Nainggolan
15	Portugal	João Mário
20	Spain	Borja Valero
44	Croatia	Ivan Perišić
77	Croatia	Marcelo Brozović
87	Italy	Antonio Candreva

FORWARDS

9	Argentina	Mauro Icardi
10	Argentina	Lautaro Martínez
11	Senegal	Keita Baldé (on loan from Monaco)
16	Italy	Matteo Politano (on loan from Sassuolo)
61	Argentina	Facundo Colidio
66	Italy	Andre Adorante

Ivan Perišić

JUVENTUS

ITALY

FOUNDED: 1897

OFFICIAL NAME: JUVENTUS FOOTBALL CLUB S.P.A.

NICKNAME: LA VECCHIA SIGNORA (THE OLD LADY)

HOME STADIUM: ALLIANZ STADIUM

OPENED: 2011

CAPACITY: 41,507

RECORD ATTENDANCE: 41,495 (AGAINST INTER MILAN IN 2018)

Allianz Stadium

HISTORY

In 1897, a few students from Torino founded Sport-Club Juventus, but the club was renamed Juventus F.C. two years later. At first, the team played in pink and black uniforms, but changed to striped black and white in 1905. The team still plays in black and white today, but the pink also shows up from time to time.

The owner of the car manufacturer FIAT, Edoardo Agnelli, acquired Juventus in 1923, and the club is still mostly owned by the Agnelli family. This is the longest-lasting relationship between a company and a sports club in history. With the purchase, Juventus became the first professional team in Italy. The increased funds allowed Juventus to win its first national league title in 1926, which was only the beginning of its continuous hoarding of major titles. Juventus is the most victorious team in Italy's history, with 34 league titles, 13 cup titles, and a total of nine European titles. Juventus is also the only team in the world that has won every possible UEFA trophy.

Juventus has remained in the top league, Serie A, since 1900, aside from the 2006–2007 season. When a big scandal shook the Italian soccer industry and five teams were accused of major fraud, Juventus was relegated to the second division as a result and many of the team's best players left. Juventus quickly recovered lost ground and was back in Serie A in no time, winning the league for eight consecutive years between 2012 and 2019!

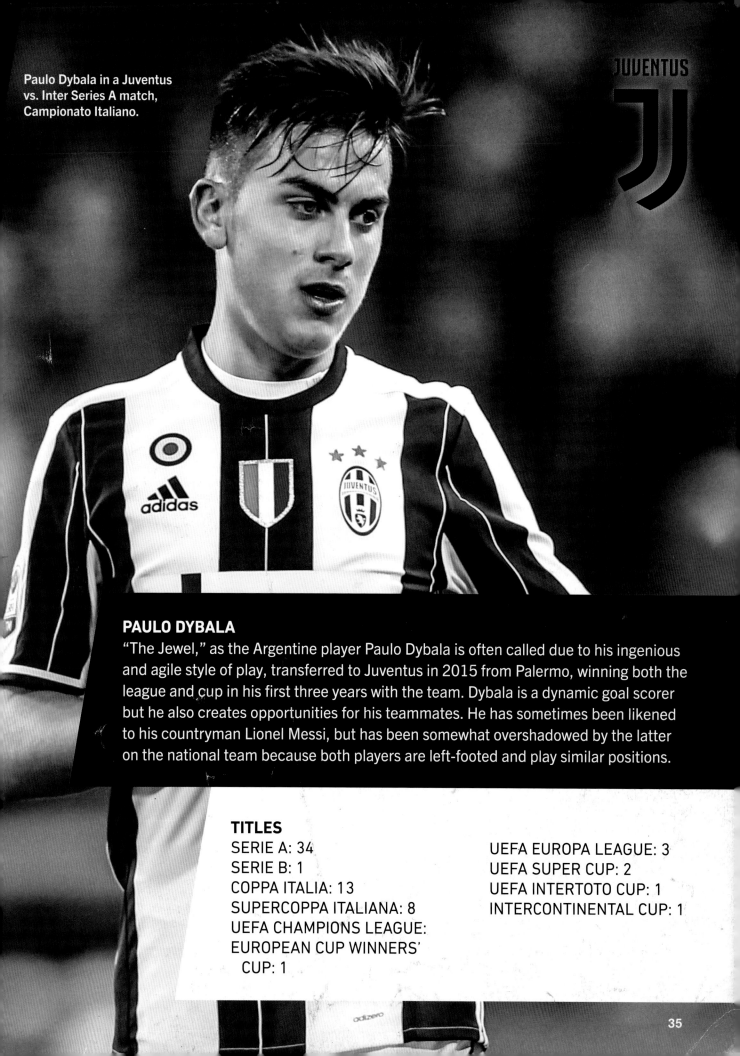

Paulo Dybala in a Juventus vs. Inter Series A match, Campionato Italiano.

PAULO DYBALA

"The Jewel," as the Argentine player Paulo Dybala is often called due to his ingenious and agile style of play, transferred to Juventus in 2015 from Palermo, winning both the league and cup in his first three years with the team. Dybala is a dynamic goal scorer but he also creates opportunities for his teammates. He has sometimes been likened to his countryman Lionel Messi, but has been somewhat overshadowed by the latter on the national team because both players are left-footed and play similar positions.

TITLES

SERIE A: 34
SERIE B: 1
COPPA ITALIA: 13
SUPERCOPPA ITALIANA: 8
UEFA CHAMPIONS LEAGUE:
EUROPEAN CUP WINNERS'
  CUP: 1

UEFA EUROPA LEAGUE: 3
UEFA SUPER CUP: 2
UEFA INTERTOTO CUP: 1
INTERCONTINENTAL CUP: 1

MOST FAMOUS PLAYERS

ALESSANDRO DEL PIERO

You could say that the Italian legend Alessandro Del Piero is the face of Juventus, due to his sheer number of game appearances and goals with the team. Indeed, Del Piero holds the record for both. He began his career with Padova but joined Juventus in 1985, at the age of 19. He was with Juventus for 19 seasons, 11 of those as team captain, scoring 290 goals in 705 games. Six league trophies, Champions League winner, World Cup champion—these are only a few of the honors that he collected over a long and productive career.

MICHEL PLATINI

Despite his position as midfielder, Frenchman Michel Platini was also an accomplished goal scorer. He was the top goal scorer in the Serie A three years in a row, top scorer in the 1985 European Cup won by Juventus, and top scorer and best player of the 1984 European Championship, which he won with the French national team. He was awarded the Ballon d'Or three times and was named the sixth best player of the last century. Platini later became UEFA president, but he was banned from all soccer related activity in 2015 for corruption charges and ethical violations.

GIANLUIGI BUFFON

Gianluigi Buffon has made the most appearances ever with the Italian national team, and many consider him the best goalkeeper of all time. He transferred to Juventus in 2001 and was part of the team for 16 seasons, winning the league a record nine times. He was named as the FIFA World Player of the Year in 2006, when Italy claimed the world championship trophy, as well as being chosen the best player of Serie A! The only honor missing from Buffon's collection is the Champions League title; he has had to settle for second place three times so far.

THE TEAM TODAY

Juventus seems to be Italy's best team at the moment. The team has won the league for the last eight years and the cup for four consecutive years. However, the wait for the next European title is growing longer. The team's last big victory was the UEFA Intertoto Cup in 1999, and in recent years, Juventus has twice been runners-up in the Champions League. Supporters hoped that the arrival of Portuguese superstar Cristiano Ronaldo would rocket the team to the title, given that Ronaldo had won the Champions League title three years in a row with Real Madrid. Nevertheless, during Ronaldo's first season, the team was eliminated in the quarterfinals by Ajax, which proved a great disappointment. Juventus has strong players in every position and will undoubtedly continue its struggle for the Champions League trophy in the years to come.

Coach: Massimiliano Allegri

GOALKEEPERS

1	Poland	Wojciech Szczęsny
21	Italy	Carlo Pinsoglio
22	Italy	Mattia Perin

DEFENDERS

2	Italy	Mattia De Sciglio
3	Italy	Giorgio Chiellini (captain)
4	Uruguay	Martín Cáceres (Lazio)
12	Brazil	Alex Sandro
15	Italy	Andrea Barzagli
19	Italy	Leonardo Bonucci
20	Portugal	João Cancelo
24	Italy	Daniele Rugani
37	Italy	Leonardo Spinazzola

MIDFIELDERS

5	B&H	Miralem Pjanić
6	Germany	Sami Khedira
14	France	Blaise Matuidi
16	Colombia	Juan Cuadrado
23	Germany	Emre Can
30	Uruguay	Rodrigo Bentancur

FORWARDS

7	Portugal	Cristiano Ronaldo
10	Argentina	Paulo Dybala
11	Brazil	Douglas Costa
17	Croatia	Mario Mandžukić
18	Italy	Moise Kean
33	Italy	Federico Bernardeschi

Cristiano Ronaldo

LIVERPOOL

ENGLAND

FOUNDED: 1892

OFFICIAL NAME: LIVERPOOL FOOTBALL CLUB

NICKNAME: THE REDS

HOME STADIUM: ANFIELD

OPENED: 1884

CAPACITY: 54,074

RECORD ATTENDANCE: 61,905 (AGAINST WOLVERHAMPTON WANDERERS IN 1952)

Anfield

HISTORY

In 1982, when the Liverpool team Everton moved its home ground from Anfield, the owner of the land, John Houlding, simply established a new soccer club and named it Everton Athletic. However, the official soccer association in England forbade Houlding from keeping the name, so he chose Liverpool F.C. instead. Liverpool won English championships in 1901, 1906, 1922, and 1923, but would not hold up another trophy until 1947. Liverpool then dropped from the top league in 1954, a downfall which took years to recover from. In 1959, Bill Shankly was hired as coach and immediately set to rebuilding the team—which involved letting go of 24 players!

Liverpool made its way back to the top league in 1962 and finally reclaimed the trophy in 1964. It then won the FA Cup for the first time a year later. The team won both the UEFA Cup and league titles in 1973, as well as the FA Cup in the following year. Shankly retired shortly after that and was replaced by his former assistant coach Bob Paisly. Paisly served as Liverpool coach for nine seasons, amassing 21 trophies over that period. In 1984, Liverpool achieved a treble, which means the team won three trophies in one season: the First Division league, FA Cup, and the UEFA Cup with coach Joe Fagan at the helm.

Kenny Dalglish led Liverpool for 1985–1990, and under his command the team won three league titles, the most recent one in 1990. From then on the team's successes began to dwindle. For close to 30 years now, Liverpool has yet to regain its old victorious stride. The high point in this dark period has been winning the UEFA Champions League, with Rafael Benítez as coach in 2005.

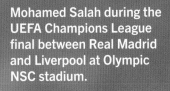

Mohamed Salah during the UEFA Champions League final between Real Madrid and Liverpool at Olympic NSC stadium.

MOHAMED SALAH

The lightning-quick Mo Salah had fallen off the radar of most English teams following a disappointing period with Chelsea in 2013–2014. Then Salah's performance improved significantly with the Italian teams Fiorentina and Roma, and Jürgen Klopp invited him to join Liverpool in 2017. During his first year with Liverpool, he became the top goal scorer in the history of the English league, with 32 goals spanning 38 seasons. Salah has maintained his finishing stride, and it will be interesting to see how far this 26-year-old player will go in the world of soccer.

TITLES

PREMIER LEAGUE: 18	FA COMMUNITY SHIELD: 15
FIRST DIVISION: 4	UEFA CHAMPIONS LEAGUE: 5
FA CUP: 7	UEFA CUP: 3
EFL CUP: 8	UEFA SUPER CUP: 3

MOST FAMOUS PLAYERS

LUIS SUÁREZ

Calling Uruguayan player Luis Suárez a wildcard would be an understatement. He has bitten his opponents three times during play and was once suspended for racial slurs. It is nevertheless hard to deny that he is one of the world's leading contemporary players, and his talents really shone with Liverpool. He scored 69 goals in 110 games, and the team's supporters were greatly saddened when Barcelona acquired him in 2014.

RAY CLEMENCE

Probably Liverpool's greatest goalkeeper and considered by many the best goalkeeper of all time, Ray Clemence played over 1,000 games for Schunthorpe United, Liverpool, and Tottenham. With Liverpool, Clemence won the league five times, the FA Cup and League Cup once each, and a total of six European Cups.

STEVEN GERRARD

Steven Gerrard will never be accused of disloyalty to his team, given that he played the entirety of his career with Liverpool (aside from a brief stint in the United States). Gerrard started out with Liverpool's youth academy at age nine and played his first game for the team at 18. He won the FA Cup twice and scored the first goal of a stunning comeback during the 2005 Champions League final when Liverpool went from 0–3 against Milan to a 3–3 tie. Gerrard's biggest regret is most likely that he retired before getting the chance to win the English Premier League.

THE TEAM TODAY

Liverpool is considered one of the world's most dynamic and entertaining soccer teams. Under the auspices of coach Jürgen Klopp, the team has come to be characterized for its powerful attacking spirit, where Mohamed Salah, Sadio Mané, and Roberto Firmino lead the energetic offense. Klopp has yet to clinch a title with the team, but fans are optimistic that it is only a matter of time. The team's lineup is rapidly improving, and with the arrival of players like the goalkeeper Alisson and the defender Virgil van Dijk, the team's defense is stronger than ever. With all positions secured, Liverpool should have the confidence to repeat its last triumph, the 2012 EFL Cup win.

Coach: Jürgen Klopp

GOALKEEPERS

13	Brazil	Alisson
22	Belgium	Simon Mignolet
62	Ireland	Caoimhin Kelleher

DEFENDERS

4	Netherlands	Virgil van Dijk
6	Croatia	Dejan Lovren
12	England	Joe Gomez
18	Spain	Alberto Moreno
26	Scotland	Andrew Robertson
32	Cameroon	Joël Matip
47	England	Nathaniel Phillips
66	England	Trent Alexander-Arnold

MIDFIELDERS

3	Brazil	Fabinno
5	Netherlands	Georginio Wijnaldum
7	England	James Milner
8	Guinea MF	Naby Keïta
14	England	Jordan Henderson (captain)
20	England	Adam Lallana
21	England	Alex Oxlade-Chamberlain
23	Switzerland	Xherdan Shaqiri
48	England	Curtis Jones
64	Portugal	Rafael Camacho

FORWARDS

9	Brazil	Roberto Firmino
10	Senegal	Sadio Mané
11	Egypt	Mohamed Salah
15	England	Daniel Sturridge
24	England	Rhian Brewster
27	Belgium	Divock Origi
58	Wales	Ben Woodburn

Jürgen Klopp

MANCHESTER CITY

ENGLAND

FOUNDED: 1897

OFFICIAL NAME: MANCHESTER CITY FOOTBALL CLUB

NICKNAMES: CITIZENS, SKY BLUES

HOME STADIUM: ETIHAD STADIUM

OPENED: 2003

CAPACITY: 55,097

RECORD ATTENDANCE: 54,693 (AGAINST LEICESTER CITY 2016)

Etihad Stadium

HISTORY

Members of a Manchester church founded the soccer club St. Mark's (West Gordon) in 1880, but renamed it Manchester City in 1894. Under that name the team won its first title, the 1904 FA Cup. The subsequent two years were difficult. The club's finances were investigated on suspicion of possible fraud, and a fire consumed the main stand by the team's Hyde Road ground. The 1930s saw major improvements as the team won another FA Cup in 1934 and, on the way to the final, Manchester City broke the English record for spectator attendance, when 85,569 people filled up the Maine Road stadium, a record that remains to this day!

Manchester City won the first league championship title in 1937 but fell from the First Division the following year. In 1956, City won the FA Cup again but once again found itself demoted from the top league. The team quickly recovered and took home the second league

trophy in 1968, followed by the FA Cup in 1969 and then the League Cup in 1970. That same year, Manchester City also won the European Cup Winners' Cup. The team continued its fight for the top titles in the following years, which yielded only one trophy, the League Cup in 1976.

It is safe to say that the next few decades were turbulent for Manchester City. The team was dropped again and again from the top league, reaching rock bottom in 1986 when it fell to the third tier. It managed once again to rise to the top, and, with the purchase of the team by Abu Dhabi United Group in 2008 and the concurrent injection of funds, Manchester City has won three Premier League titles, the FA Cup once, and the EFL Cup four times.

Sergio "Kun" Agüero smiles before a game.

SERGIO AGÜERO

Sergio Agüero had only been 15 years old for 35 days when he played his first game in the top league in Argentina, beating Diego Maradona's record. In 2006, he joined Atlético Madrid and from there transferred to Manchester City in 2011. During the final of his first season in England, Agüero scored the winning goal against QPR, securing the team's first league title in 44 years. He is Manchester City's all-time top goal scorer, the top-scoring South American player in the English league, and the fifth player in Premier League history to score five goals in a single game.

TITLES

PREMIER LEAGUE: 5	FA COMMUNITY SHIELD: 5
FIRST DIVISION: 7	EUROPEAN CUP WINNERS'
FA CUP: 5	CUP: 1
EFL CUP: 6	

MOST FAMOUS PLAYERS

COLIN BELL

It is not without reason that the West Stand of the Etihad Stadium is named after Colin Bell, one the finest players in the history of Manchester City. Bell played midfield and was the key to City's success in the 1960s. He scored over 100 goals and won a total of five titles with the team. Unfortunately, injury put an end to Bell's career, and the team has since then struggled to find his heir.

YAYA TOURÉ

When it comes to box-to-box midfielders with all-round abilities, assisting both defenders and forwards as well as readily assuming both positions themselves, there are few who come close to the talents of Yaya Touré from the Ivory Coast. He breaks up one offensive drive after another and then darts across the field with the ball to create dangerous opportunities for teammates. Following brief travels around Europe, Touré transferred to Barcelona where he won seven titles in two years, before joining City in 2010, adding another seven titles to the collection.

DAVID SILVA

Spanish player David Silva is one of the key components in Manchester City's recent climb to success. Silva transferred from Valencia in 2010 and has contributed his efforts toward all the team's titles over the last years. The cunning playmaker creates countless opportunities for his teammates and regularly scores goals himself, evidenced by the fact that Silva is the fourth top goal scorer of the Spanish national team since its inception. With the national team, Silva won three consecutive major tournaments: 2008 UEFA European Championship, 2010 World Cup, and the UEFA European Championship again in 2012.

THE TEAM TODAY

After the club was bought by Abu Dhabi Group, Manchester City has progressed immensely. In 2012 the team won the league for the first time in 44 years and then repeated the feat in 2014. One of the world's leading coaches, Pep Guardiola, was hired in 2016. With Guardiola at the helm, the team won the league championship in 2018, beating a number of records that season: No other team has scored the same amount of points (100), scored more goals (106), won more games (32), and so on and so forth.

Manchester City should have no problem building on these triumphs, and if the ownership remains the same with a steady flow of money, the team will keep acquiring the world's top soccer players and very best coaches. The main disappointment for supporters is the team's recent performance in the UEFA Champions League, and in 2019, City was defeated by Tottenham during the quarterfinals, a result that few could have foreseen.

Coach: Pep Guardiola

Raheem Sterling

GOALKEEPERS

1	Chile	Claudio Bravo
31	Brazil	Ederson
32	England	Daniel Grimshaw
49	Kosovo	Arijanet Muric

DEFENDERS

2	England	Kyle Walker
3	Brazil	Danilo
4	Belgium	Vincent Kompany (captain)
5	England	John Stones
14	France	Aymeric Laporte
15	France	Eliaquim Mangala
22	France	Benjamin Mendy
30	Argentina	Nicolás Otamendi
34	Netherlands	Philippe Sandler

MIDFIELDERS

8	Germany	İlkay Gündoğan
17	Belgium	Kevin De Bruyne
18	England	Fabian Delph
19	Germany	Leroy Sané
20	Portugal	Bernardo Silva
21	Spain	David Silva
25	Brazil	Fernandinho
26	Algeria	Riyad Mahrez
35	Ukraine	Oleksandr Zinchenko
47	England	Phil Foden

FORWARDS

7	England	Raheem Sterling
10	Argentina	Sergio Agüero
33	Brazil	Gabriel Jesus

MANCHESTER UNITED

ENGLAND

FOUNDED: 1878

OFFICIAL NAME: MANCHESTER UNITED FOOTBALL CLUB

NICKNAME: THE RED DEVILS

HOME STADIUM: OLD TRAFFORD

OPENED: 1910

CAPACITY: 74,994

RECORD ATTENDANCE: 76,962 (WOLVERHAMPTON WANDERERS AGAINST GRIMSBY TOWN IN 1939)

Old Trafford

HISTORY

In 1978, a few employees of a railway company in Manchester established a soccer club and named it Newton Heath LYR. The first years were difficult, and by 1903 the club had fallen into such debt that one member was forced to ask around town for people willing to invest. Four local businessmen decided to sponsor the team with 500 pounds each, and the club was given a new name as a result: Manchester United.

The team performed pretty well in the beginning of the 20th century, for example, with a First Division championship in 1908 and the FA Cup a year later. However, the next few years would see uneven performances, with the team yo-yoing between the First and Second Division leagues. It was not until Matt Busby took over as coach in 1945 that the team finally established itself as a proper powerhouse. The team won the FA Cup and then the First Division title, and Manchester United became the first English team to participate in the European Cup, where it went on to crush the Belgian legends in Anderlecht 10–0.

On February 6, 1958, an airplane carrying the Manchester United team crashed in Munich, resulting in 23 casualties, among them eight players. The team eventually worked through the tragedy and in 1968, still led by Busby, became the first English team to win the European Cup. After Busby retired in 1969, the team's performance in the league began to waver, but it managed to clinch the FA Cup a few times. Scottish coach Alex Ferguson was then hired in 1986 and, under his command, Manchester United became England's most triumphant team. With Ferguson, the team won the Premier League 13 times, the FA Cup five times, and the UEFA Champions League twice, to name but a few of the highlights.

George Best at the height of his career.

GEORGE BEST

Many soccer specialists claim that Northern Irish player George Best was one of the very best players of all time. The quick and agile winger would send his opponents into a spin as he dribbled through their defense. Best helped Manchester United win its first European title in 1968, and in the same year he was chosen the world's greatest soccer player.

TITLES

PREMIER LEAGUE: 20

FIRST DIVISION: 2

FA CUP: 12

EFL CUP: 5

FA COMMUNITY SHIELD: 21

UEFA CHAMPIONS LEAGUE: 3

UEFA CUP WINNERS' CUP: 1

UEFA EUROPA LEAGUE: 1

UEFA SUPER CUP: 1

INTERCONTINENTAL CUP: 1

FIFA CLUB WORLD CUP: 1

MOST FAMOUS PLAYERS

BOBBY CHARLTON

Bobby Charlton spent almost his entire career with Manchester United. He was the team's second all-time goal scorer with 249 goals. With United, Charlton won the league three times and the FA Cup and UEFA Champions League once each. As a member of the English national team, he won the 1966 World Cup and was selected the world's best player the same year. He was known for his speed, passing abilities, and long shots that led to numerous goals.

RYAN GIGGS

No player in history has amassed as many titles and honors with his team as Ryan Giggs. With Manchester United, he won 34 titles, for example, 13 league titles, four FA Cup titles, and two UEFA Champions League titles. Giggs, a cunning left winger, played his first top league game at only 17 and was soon offered a professional contract with the team. Giggs, along with players like David Beckham, Paul Scholes, and brothers Gary and Phil Neville, are part of the generation of players who graduated from the youth academy as "Class of '92."

WAYNE ROONEY

Not only is Wayne Rooney the all-time goal scorer of Manchester United, but he is also the top goal scorer in the history of the English national team. Rooney became the youngest player ever to score a goal in the Premier League: five days before he turned 17, he scored for his favorite team Everton in a game against Arsenal. Manchester United acquired him at the age of 19, where he would begin his vast trophy collection.

THE TEAM TODAY

Following Alex Ferguson's retirement, the team has struggled with maintaining its former successful streak in the top league. David Moyes was hired as coach in 2013 but only lasted 10 months in the position. Louis van Gaal was picked up in his stead, and despite claiming the FA Cup, he was let go after only two seasons in light of the team's overall disappointing performance. José Mourinho was then brought on board to revamp United, and though he helped the team win the first Champions League title as well as the FA Cup, Mourinho only managed one and a half seasons.

When a former Manchester United player, Ole Gunnar Solskjær, was named coach, the team's performance improved dramatically. Manchester United won the first eight games and eliminated the star-studded PSG during the Round of 16 of the UEFA Champions League, despite having previously lost 0–2 on home ground. Solskjær was awarded for his good start with a three-year contract, and now it will be interesting to see whether Man U has found a coach that will last more than two years.

Coach: Ole Gunnar Solskjær

Paul Pogba

GOALKEEPERS

1	Spain	David de Gea
13	England	Lee Grant
22	Argentina	Sergio Romero

DEFENDERS

2	Sweden	Victor Lindelöf
3	Ivory Coast	Eric Bailly
4	England	Phil Jones
12	England	Chris Smalling
16	Argentina	Marcos Rojo
18	England	Ashley Young
20	Portugal	Diogo Dalot
23	England	Luke Shaw
25	Ecuador	Antonio Valencia (captain)
36	Italy	Matteo Darmian

MIDFIELDERS

6	France	Paul Pogba
8	Spain	Juan Mata
14	England	Jesse Lingard
15	Brazil	Andreas Pereira
17	Brazil	Fred
21	Spain	Ander Herrera
31	Serbia	Nemanja Matić
39	Scotland	Scott McTominay

FORWARDS

7	Chile	Alexis Sánchez
9	Belgium	Romelu Lukaku
10	England	Marcus Rashford
11	France	Anthony Martial

PARIS SAINT-GERMAIN

FRANCE

FOUNDED: 1970

OFFICIAL NAME: PARIS SAINT-GERMAIN
FOOTBALL CLUB

NICKNAMES: LES PARISIENS (THE
PARISIANS), LES ROUGE ET BLEU (THE
RED AND BLUES)

HOME STADIUM: PARC DES PRINCES

OPENED: 1972

CAPACITY: 47,929

RECORD ATTENDANCE: 50,370 (FRANCE
AGAINST WALES IN 1989)

Parc Des Princes

HISTORY

On August 12, 1970, the Parisian clubs Paris Football Club and Stade-Saint Germain merged into one club, called Saint-Germain Football Club. The team rose quickly and leapt from the second division to the top national league, Ligue 1, in the first year. In 1972, the team was divided again, but the part that kept the PSG name was forced to begin in the third division. PSG was back in Ligue 1 in only two years, and this has been the team's home ever since. It is the only team in France's history that has never been relegated.

PSG laid claim to its first title in 1982, winning the French Cup, and the first league title arrived four years later. PSG won another league trophy in 1994 along with a host of cup titles. No other French team has won the national cup as often

as PSG, a total of 12 times. The team's greatest achievement in Europe, came in 1996 with a victory in the UEFA Cup Winners' Cup.

The going got tougher in the 21st century and PSG just barely avoided relegation. The tides changed when the club was bought by Qatar Sports Investments, making it one of the world's richest. Since 2013, PSG has won the league six times in seven years as well as the national cup almost every season. Despite its relatively short history, the team holds a variety of national records, for example, the record for most titles won and most consecutive seasons in Ligue 1.

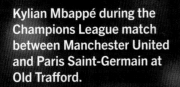
Kylian Mbappé during the Champions League match between Manchester United and Paris Saint-Germain at Old Trafford.

KYLIAN MBAPPÉ

The young forward, Kylian Mbappé is not considered the most promising up-and-coming players, instead, he is already one of the greatest! Mbappé was born and raised in Paris but began his professional career with Monaco, when he was only 16. He helped Monaco win the league in 2017 and then transferred to PSG for two more league titles. Mbappé became world champion with the French national team in 2018 as the second teenager in history to score in a World Cup final, after the legendary Pelé.

TITLES

LIGUE 1: 7	TROPHÉE DES CHAMPIONS: 8
LIGUE 2: 1	UEFA CUP WINNERS' CUP: 1
COUPE DE FRANCE: 12	UEFA INTERTOTO CUP: 1
COUPE DE LA LIGUE: 8	

MOST FAMOUS PLAYERS

THIAGO SILVA

When PSG acquired Brazilian player Thiago Silva from AC Milan in 2012, he was the second-most expensive midfielders of all time. Some even claim that the team paid too little, given the fact that Silva is a near-flawless defender. Fast, strong, and ingenious, but above all, a born leader, Silva is a key figure in PSG's recent rise.

SAFET SUŠIĆ

In 2010, the magazine *France Football*, mostly known for presenting the Ballon d'Or to the best players each year, selected the best players in the history of the French league. The best foreign player and PSG's best player was Bosnian Safet Sušić. This creative attacking midfielder appeared in close to 300 games for PSG and won the league title once. He also played for Yugoslavia and Bosnia and Herzegovina, and in 2004, was named the best player of the latter country.

ZLATAN IBRAHIMOVIĆ

When PSG's new owners from Qatar bought the club, they insisted on acquiring a star. That star would be Swede Zlatan Ibrahimović, who had already made a name for himself with Juventus, Inter Milan, Barcelona and AC Milan. The colorful forward is PSG's top goal scorer of all time, with 156 goals in 180 games. He is also the top scorer for the Swedish national team, with 62 goals. Ibrahimović is often considered the greatest forward of his generation.

THE TEAM TODAY

There are not many clubs in the world that can fork over as much money for players or pay as stupendous salaries as PSG can. As a result, the team is manned by top talent, despite the fact that the French league has not always been the most desirable career choice for star players. The Qatar owners have spent vast amounts of money on building a soccer empire and investigative journalists have even accused them of fraudulent behavior, but no proof has surfaced in the matter.

PSG has often declared its intention to win the Champions League title, but for some inexplicable reason, it has never managed to climb beyond the quarterfinals. In 2019, PSG was eliminated by Manchester United in the Round of 16, despite having defeated the team 0—2 in the previous game at Old Trafford. Of course, PSG maintains its triumphant reign in the top French league; however, it is clear that if the performance in Europe doesn't improve in the next season, German coach Thomas Tuchel will have to start looking for other career options.

Coach: Thomas Tuchel

Neymar

GOALKEEPERS

1	Italy	Gianluigi Buffon
16	France	Alphonse Areola
50	France	Sebastien Cibois

DEFENDERS

2	Brazil	Thiago Silva (captain)
3	France	Presnel Kimpembe
4	Germany	Thilo Kehrer
5	Brazil	Marquinhos
12	Belgium	Thomas Meunier
13	Brazil	Dani Alves
14	Spain	Juan Bernat
20	France	Layvin Kurzawa
31	France	Colin Dagba
34	France	Stanley Nsoki

MIDFIELDERS

6	Italy	Marco Verratti
8	Argentina	Leandro Paredes
11	Argentina	Ángel Di María
23	Germany	Julian Draxler
24	France	Christopher Nkunku
25	France	Adrien Rabiot

FORWARDS

7	France	Kylian Mbappé
9	Uruguay	Edinson Cavani
10	Brazil	Neymar
17	Cameroon	Eric Maxim Choupo-Moting
27	France	Moussa Diaby

REAL MADRID

SPAIN

FOUNDED: 1902

OFFICIAL NAME: REAL MADRID CLUB DE FÚTBOL

NICKNAMES: LOS BLANCOS (THE WHITES), LOS MERENGUES (THE MERINGUES)

HOME STADIUM: ESTADIO SANTIAGO BERNABÉU

OPENED: 1947

CAPACITY: 81,044

RECORD ATTENDANCE: 129,690 (AGAINST AC MILAN IN 1956)

Estadio Santiago Bernabéu

HISTORY

British students introduced the game of soccer to Madrid around the turn of the 20th century. In 1902, former members of the soccer team Sky Football came together and established a new team, which was named Madrid FC. The new team won the Spanish Cup in 1905. The name was changed to Real Madrid after King Alfonso XIII gave the team the title "Real," which means royal in Spanish and explains the crown that embellishes Real Madrid's emblem.

Real Madrid won the Spanish league in 1932 and 1933, but the team would not become a soccer behemoth until the 1950s. The first Champions League tournament (then known as the European Cup) was held in 1956, and Real Madrid won the first five years in a row! In 1966, Real Madrid won the cup for the sixth time, now manned by only Spanish players, which marked the first time ever that a team with only native players won the trophy.

Real is one of three teams that has never been relegated from top-level Spanish play in La Liga, nor has the team experienced any particular low point in its history. Real Madrid regularly wins La Liga and the Spanish Cup, as its collection of Champions League trophies grows and grows. Soccer stars continue to arrive in droves to join Real's ranks and prove their worth with one of Europe's greatest soccer clubs.

Cristiano Ronaldo during the UEFA Champions League final between Real Madrid and Liverpool.

CRISTIANO RONALDO

There is only one person who can possibly prevent Cristiano Ronaldo from claiming the title of the world's greatest living soccer player—none other than Ronaldo's archenemy Lionel Messi. Ronaldo helped Manchester United win the UEFA Champions League in 2008 and the Premier League three times before moving on to join Real Madrid. There, Ronaldo clinched four additional titles in top tournaments, as well as becoming a European champion with Portugal in 2016. Ronaldo is now with Juventus and will no doubt continue to amass honors.

TITLES

LA LIGA: 33	UEFA EUROPA LEAGUE: 2
COPA DEL REY: 19	UEFA SUPER CUP: 4
SUPERCOPA DE ESPAÑA: 10	INTERCONTINENTAL CUP: 3
UEFA CHAMPIONS LEAGUE: 13	FIFA CLUB WORLD CUP: 4

MOST FAMOUS PLAYERS

RONALDO

Cristiano is not the only Ronaldo to have made a dazzling impression in the white uniform. Between 2002 and 2007, it was the Brazilian Ronaldo that charmed the supporters of Real Madrid. With true grace and his characteristic technical abilities, Ronaldo danced past his opponents and racked up glorious goals. He also played for Real's rivals in Barcelona, and in Italy, Ronaldo played with two teams that also share a heated history: Inter Milan and AC Milan.

ZINEDINE ZIDANE

Before Zidane became one the world's finest coaches, he was considered by many to be the best attacking midfielder the game had ever witnessed. He played with Cannes and Bordeaux in France before transferring to Juventus. He won the top league title with Juventus before being acquired by Real Madrid for a record amount. With Real he claimed the league title as well as the Champions League trophy. In the Champions League final, Zidane scored a goal which is viewed by many as the most beautiful in the tournament's history. With the French national team, he won both the World Cup and the European Championship.

IKER CASILLAS

Few have served Real Madrid and the Spanish national team with the same dexterity as "Saint Iker" Casilla. He has made the second-highest number of appearances in the history of Real Madrid and played a record of 167 games for the Spanish national team. This powerful goalkeeper has won numerous titles, both with clubs and the national team. It is certain that Real Madrid would have fewer trophies if not for Saint Iker's service.

THE TEAM TODAY

In 2017, Real Madrid became the first team in history to win the UEFA Champions League for two consecutive years after the tournament was rebranded in 1992. Winning the tournament again in 2018 was therefore an amazing achievement. Coach Zinedine Zidane retired following the win, and the team's brightest star, Cristiano Ronaldo, left for Juventus. Real's performance plummeted as a result, and two coaches, Julen Lopetegui and Santiago Solari, were fired in one season. Zinedine Zidane has been rehired in the hopes that he can bring back the former glory and build another superstar team hungry for championship titles!

Coach: Zinedine Zidane

Gareth Bale

GOALKEEPERS

1	Costa Rica	Keylor Navas
25	Belgium	Thibaut Courtois
30	France	Luca Zidane

DEFENDERS

2	Spain	Dani Carvajal
3	Spain	Jesús Vallejo
4	Spain	Sergio Ramos (captain)
5	France	Raphaël Varane
6	Spain	Nacho
12	Brazil	Marcelo
19	Spain	Álvaro Odriozola
23	Spain	Sergio Reguilón

MIDFIELDERS

8	Germany	Toni Kroos
10	Croatia	Luka Modrić
14	Brazil	Casemiro
15	Uruguay	Fede Valverde
18	Spain	Marcos Llorente
20	Spain	Marco Asensio
21	Spain	Brahim Díaz
22	Spain	Isco
24	Spain	Dani Ceballos

FORWARDS

7	Dominican Republic	Mariano Díaz
9	France	Karim Benzema
11	Wales	Gareth Bale
17	Spain	Lucas Vázquez
28	Brazil	Vinícius Júnior

TOTTENHAM

ENGLAND

FOUNDED: 1882

OFFICIAL NAME: TOTTENHAM HOTSPUR FOOTBALL CLUB

NICKNAMES: SPURS, THE LILYWHITES

HOME STADIUM: TOTTENHAM HOTSPUR STADIUM

OPENED: 2019

CAPACITY: 62,062

RECORD ATTENDANCE: 60,044 (AGAINST MANCHESTER CITY IN 2019)

Tottenham Hotspur Stadium

HISTORY

The soccer club Tottenham Hotspur was established in 1882 by a number of young cricket players who were looking for sports activities during the wintertime. The team grew quickly in the first years and became a fully professional team in 1895. Tottenham won the FA Cup in 1901, the only team to have claimed the trophy without being part of the top English league (Tottenham later joined in 1908). The team traveled rough seas until the 1950s, swinging between the First and the Second Division, but in 1951, the team finally claimed the English championship title.

In 1961, Tottenham was the first team in the 20th century to take a League and FA Cup Double, winning both league and cup trophies, with another FA Cup win in the following year. The team then came out on top in the European Cup Winners' Cup, the first British team ever to claim this honor. Tottenham was also the first British team to win two European Cups, taking home the UEFA Cup trophy in 1972.

Tottenham has struggled to win the league since then but managed another UEFA Cup title in 1984. The team continued to amass FA Cup titles, and in 1991, Tottenham was the first team to win eight FA trophies. Despite having some of the world's best soccer players on board, the team has failed to snatch another top title since

TOTTENHAM HOTSPUR

HARRY KANE

It is strange but true that Harry Kane was kicked out of Arsenal's youth academy for being slightly overweight. He joined Tottenham's academy when he was 11 but did not make much of an impression, aside from his diligence and determination. But these traits would certainly pay off during his first season with Tottenham, when he scored 31 goals! Since then, he has twice been the Premier League's top goal scorer, once during the World Cup, and six times been player of the month in the Premier League, an honor Kane shares with Steven Gerrard.

TITLES

PREMIER LEAGUE: 2

FIRST DIVISION: 2

FA CUP: 8

EFL CUP: 4

FA COMMUNITY SHIELD: 7

UEFA CUP WINNERS' CUP: 1

UEFA EUROPA LEAGUE: 2

MOST FAMOUS PLAYERS

GARETH BALE

Bale began his career as a left back with Southampton and was then acquired by Tottenham when he was only 18 years old. With Tottenham, Bale was given a position closer to the opponent's goal as an attacking midfielder or winger. He was a key player on the team during that time and was named the PFA Players' Player of the Year in 2013. Real Madrid then acquired Bale for a record sum, and he has won four major titles with that team, to name a few achievements. Bale is the top goal-scorer of all time for the Welsh national team.

PAUL GASCOIGNE

Gazza, as Paul Gascoigne is often called, is one of the most talented soccer players in England's history. The attacking midfielder had it all: speed, strength, agility, endurance. But above all, he racked up countless goals through his intelligent style of play. Gazza is a colorful character and would stop only briefly with teams, but while playing for Tottenham, he was a fan favorite, especially when the team won the FA Cup in 1991.

GARY LINEKER

One of England's greatest strikers, Gary Lineker, was awarded the Golden Boot at the 1986 World Cup and was the only Englishman to have achieved this until Harry Kane claimed the same honor in 2018. He is also the only player to have become the top goal scorer in the Premier League with three different teams, with Leicester, Everton, and Tottenham. Despite a long career defined by a fighting spirit, Lineker never got a yellow or red card!

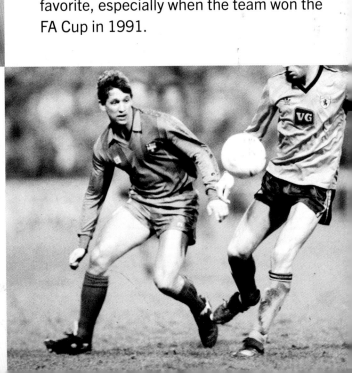

THE TEAM TODAY

Coach Mauricio Pochettino was hired by Tottenham in 2014 and has managed to build a powerful new team, manned by players like Harry Kane and Christian Eriksen. The team came in second in the Premier League in 2017, Tottenham's first major success in the league since 1963. The team made it to the Champions League semifinals of this season, and it is clear that if Tottenham manages to keep its top players, the next few years will be an exciting time in the newly constructed home stadium, Tottenham Hotspur Stadium, one of the world's most amazing sports arenas. Meanwhile, the team's supporters will continue to dream about the next title.

Coach: Mauricio Pochettino

GOALKEEPERS

1	France	Hugo Lloris (captain)
13	Netherlands	Michel Vorm
22	Argentina	Paulo Gazzaniga

DEFENDERS

2	England	Kieran Trippier
3	England	Danny Rose
4	Belgium	Toby Alderweireld
5	Belgium	Jan Vertonghen
6	Colombia	Davinson Sánchez
16	England	Kyle Walker-Peters
21	Argentina	Juan Foyth
24	Ivory Coast	Serge Aurier
33	Wales	Ben Davies

MIDFIELDERS

8	England	Harry Winks
11	Argentina	Erik Lamela
12	Kenya	Victor Wanyama
15	England	Eric Dier
17	France	Moussa Sissoko
20	England	Dele Alli
23	Denmark	Christian Eriksen
27	Brazil	Lucas Moura

FORWARDS

7	South Korea	Son Heung-min
10	England	Harry Kane
18	Spain	Fernando Llorente
—	Netherlands	Vincent Janssen

Son Heung-min

Liverpool players celebrate a hard-won victory at the UEFA Champions League Final in Madrid on June 1, 2019.